D1577387

CANTERBURY

The rivers, over and over again the rivers
They hasten to you, look up them, in the riverbeds.
From the soft dark forest they come down,
Or from the snows, carving their patterns
Of tawny terraces they come hastening down
To where by archipelagos of silver,
Lizard twists of azure, tranced lagoons,
We hear the ripples and the silence sing together
With the small soft sighing of the tussock,
And the flax spears' rattle and, might be, a seabird's call.

– from 'By the River Ashley' by Ursula Bethell

CANTERBURY

PHOTOGRAPHY ARNO GASTEIGER INTRODUCTION PHILIP TEMPLE

VIKING

An imprint of
PENGUIN BOOKS

ACKNOWLEDGEMENTS

Canterbury is the third book in a series that explores remarkable provinces of New Zealand. I enjoyed working with the team at Penguin Books and would like to give my special thanks to Bernice Beachman for all her help.

Covering such a huge and diverse area as Canterbury proved to be a challenge. I felt it necessary to include some of the unique architecture, but did not want to interrupt the seamless flow of what is really a book of landscapes.

I greatly value the help of my wife and picture editor, Sue. This wonderful presentation was achieved through the skilful design by Athena Sommerfeld. Philip Temple is a knowledgeable writer and I am thankful for his contribution.

Many thanks also to Gary Baildon and Anthony Corban from FUJIFILM NZ Ltd for their continuing generous support.

Finally, I thank the people of Canterbury, who shared their knowledge and enthusiasm for this special place.

INTRODUCTION
PHILIP TEMPLE

WE PUT OUT FROM LYTTELTON, BEATING INTO A STIFF OLD-MAN EASTERLY THAT FLICKED THE WHITE-CAPS ALL THE WAY DOWN THE HARBOUR.

The seven-metre white sloop clawed into it well, and Gordon's soft hand on the tiller coaxed every slight advantage from wind shifts running down the flanks of the headlands. As he predicted, it took us an hour or more to make the harbour entrance, and there little Sappho began to stagger into the swells of the open ocean. When I looked back to Banks Peninsula's high lava cliffs and then north to the vast curve of Pegasus Bay, I felt as insignificant as a gull and a good deal more vulnerable. But Sappho was well found, she and Gordon had done this before, and the marine forecast was good. I took the tiller, while Gordon fussed with ropes and sails, and I held the port tack, making more sea room. A couple of miles offshore, I turned Sappho's nose south and we eased the sheets, knowing the wind would follow us around the curve of the peninsula. Sappho felt freed, and I felt a surge of exhilaration as the swells now lifted us on our way: excitement sobered by anxiety, a touch of apprehension at what might lie ahead around the next bend in the coast. Not for the first time, I wondered what in the world it would have felt like to have been the first to sail this way.

When Maori voyagers first sailed their waka along this coast, scudding along, perhaps, before a similar stiff nor'easter, they were looking at a land entirely foreign to their past experience of island and atoll, volcanic peak and tropical forest. Beneath skies heavy with whales of cloud lay vast plains and big mountains that seemed topped with foam like the ocean breakers. They sailed beside something beyond easy understanding: a land too high and too wide to readily conform with the shape of another island.

A car outside the Hilltop Hotel (W. Newton, proprietor), Akaroa, c. 1910.

G 8869 1/1. Alexander Turnbull Library, Wellington, New Zealand.

The South Island is no larger than Greece but the scale of its landscapes reveal that it is less an island than the remnant of a continent – ancient Gondwana – dominated by the upthrust of the 800-kilometre-long Southern Alps. These form the Main Divide between the narrow and precipitous strip of the wild West Coast and the dry foothills, downlands and plains of the east. The island is made up of the Alps' buckle and dross, and the mountains make the weather, shape the sky and dictate the patterns of life.

The largest part of this mountain-shadowed landscape, encompassing the most considerable plains in New Zealand and its most extensive montane prairies, has become known as Canterbury. Bounded on the west by the highest peaks of the Southern Alps, on the east by endlessly curving Pacific beaches, its northern and southern margins are the long, braided rivers of the Waiau and Waitaki, two of seven great Canterbury streams that trace their source to alpine snow and ice.

As the working of the Alpine Fault continues to uplift the Southern Alps, glaciers grind them down and their rivers carry away the silt and gravel, spilling through foothill gorges to form the biggest shingle fan in the world. Banks Peninsula, jutting from the east coast like a scarred greenstone mere, was once an island, exploding from the sea as a volcano thirty million years ago when the foothills of the Alps lay across a 60-kilometre-wide strait. But over aeons, the extending fan of shingle steadily filled in the gap, and the junction was complete by the time the first Maori put ashore.

At dusk we slipped into the bay, deserted but for a single farm house, and found an overnight anchorage in the lee of the southern cliffs. For a while we put up with the lump of the dissipating easterly swell, but were soon confirmed in our judgement by the arrival of the southerly in a sudden freezing downpour that seemed to cow the surface of the bay. I looked across to a north-facing gully with its grove of old karakas: Here Maori had made a settlement centuries before and it was said they brought the karaka seeds with them from Polynesia. As the southerly set in and I lay swaddled in my sleeping bag, I could not imagine how they kept warm in such a climate.

At first, the dry forests of the plains were exploited by Maori hunters pursuing flocks of grazing moa. Fires and dogs were used to herd them into the traps of coastal estuaries where they were slaughtered on such a scale that within a few centuries this entire race of birds was extinct. After the age of moa hunting, Waitaha people were supplanted by Ngati Mamoe invading from the north and the 1000-metre-high peninsula became the most favoured locus of settlement. Much of the South Island was too cold for Polynesian settlement but the peninsula was warmer and well-watered from coastal rains, clothed in forest and margined by lagoons and swamps, all as rich in birds as the coastal seas and shores were in seals and fish. Kumara and karaka could grow in its warm bays; its headlands were suited to fortified pa. It remained an island rich in food, shelter and safe anchorage against the harder, more challenging world of dry plains and hills that swept westwards to the Alps.

By the late 18th century, Canterbury had come under the control of hapu associated with another invading tribe, Ngai Tahu, who had built their major pa at Kaiapohia (just north of today's Christchurch). A few hundred Poutini Ngai Tahu lived close to greenstone (pounamu) sources across the Southern Alps and a web of Maori routeways from Kaiapohia led to passes across the Alps, attesting to the jade's trading value. By Captain Cook's arrival, every iwi in the country had obtained the chiefly taonga of pounamu ornaments.

On his map of New Zealand, Cook showed Banks Peninsula as an island and his mistake was not discovered until 1809 when the first British sealing ship sailed by. Over the following thirty years European sealers, whalers and traders began to visit with increasing frequency and the first shore whaling stations were established on the south side of Banks Peninsula in the mid-1830s. The arrival of Europeans coincided with the self-destruction of the Ngai Tahu iwi when, in 1824, a breach of protocol against paramount chief Te Maiharanui set up a cycle of intra-tribal cannibalistic killing that became known as 'Kai huanga', the 'eat relation' feud. Around 1830, torn apart and demoralised, Ngai Tahu now became prey to Ngati Toa warrior chief Te Rauparaha who led raiding parties south across Cook Strait from his stronghold on Kapiti Island. Hundreds were killed and pa devastated as the fighting raged back and forth over the next decade. In 1820, Canterbury had a Ngai Tahu population of about 3000 people; in 1840 it was just 600, a total that was soon reduced even further by new European diseases such as measles and tuberculosis. Ngai Tahu were also now easy prey for pakeha land speculators and dictatorial government agents. By 1848, almost all of the South Island had passed to the Crown and settler landowners for a few thousand pounds. Just 2575 hectares had been reserved for the 647 Ngai Tahu still living in the southern half of the island and they had been driven off many of their traditional settlement sites. The injuries and indignities inflicted on Ngai Tahu were not recompensed until the Treaty of Waitangi settlement of 1998.

When we sailed into Akaroa Harbour under the shadow of Takitimu Head, I felt the sense of haven that all salt-caked, wind-burned mariners have felt over the years, as they turned away from the unforgiving wastes of the South Pacific and looked inwards to the promise of warm tranquillity among the verdant hills of the best harbour along the entire east coast of the South Island. As we slipped along before the dying southerly, the old town opened up to us, and it seemed as if it had been there forever, basking

Cooking class, St Margaret's College,
Christchurch, 1914.

G-4336-1/1, Alexander Turnbull Library, Wellington, New Zealand.

in the sun. It was a place to drop anchor and go ashore for a while, sailors home from the sea in a tradition carried from the other side of the world.

Akaroa became the first permanent European settlement in Canterbury when French settlers established a colony there in 1840. Although the French government hoped this might be the start of something bigger, perhaps a sovereign French colony, the enterprise was too half-hearted to succeed. When Charles Lavaud, the French Royal Commissioner, arrived in the Bay of Islands in July to herald French settlers he discovered that the Treaty of Waitangi had been signed and the whole country declared a British Crown colony. Governor William Hobson quickly sent officials to Akaroa to hold court sessions and raise the Union Jack in case Lavaud had any other ideas. The French colony never grew, mostly because there was not enough land around Akaroa suitable for agricultural development and, for many years, access was possible only by sea. For all the warmth and beauty of its location, Akaroa would forever remain a charming Gallic oasis within a Britannic New Zealand.

The empty plains were a more logical site for a new colony. In provoking the formation of the Canterbury Association – a colonising venture sponsored by Church of England leaders – Edward Gibbon Wakefield, founder of the New Zealand Company, took a last opportunity to implement his theories of colonisation. Based on planned settlements populated by all classes of society, the scheme attracted unemployed young English gentry with hopes of privileged usefulness; the shabby but genteel lower-middle-class with ideas of making a fortune; and the labouring poor attracted by the prospect of work and eventually some land of their own. For all, there was the chance of achieving that very Victorian ideal of 'improvement'.

The first Canterbury settlers arrived in Lyttelton harbour on 'The First Four Ships' just before Christmas 1850. Along with cart and plough, sickle and milk churn, they also brought English names to extinguish the Maori, along with their title to the land. 'Christchurch' was to be the chief town and 'Avon' its winding river. From the crest of the Port Hills, the settlers looked over the vast 'Canterbury Plains', dissected by the glittering braids of the great Waimakariri River and, for one mad moment, renamed it Cholmondeley ('Chumley'). They saw, according to poet Arnold Wall:

. . . league upon league, hill, plain and spur,
   Of grass of the colour of weasel's fur,
   Of leafless bushes and sedges harsh
   And ragged forest and reedy marsh . . .[1]

– where their planned city would lie. Some of the settlers 'missed the greenness . . . of a country long cultivated', but this empty country, where all was broad and high and wide, was unhedged by anything save their own minds. And they had a mind to make it a better England, to make this strange wilderness a rural paradise. The Canterbury 'pilgrims' were luckier than settlers in other parts of New Zealand who hacked at mountains for roads, struggled with heavy bush or battled with Maori. Canterbury land was tractable, the climate even and natives almost non-existent. The landscape could be redrawn or at least put firmly in its place.

Yet it took longer than expected to establish the ideal settlement of Christchurch market town, with an Anglican church establishment and schools, served by a prosperous agricultural hinterland. There were too many speculators, too few labourers and not much from which to earn an income. Cathedral, manor and a chequerboard of wheatfields became no more than a fantasy when the nearest big market was Australia and the greatest export became labour heading for goldfields across the Tasman. Little labour and less market meant a change of plan. Orderly migration, surveyed city and the right people with the right outlook were nothing without cash. The gentlemen who led the colony saw what must be done. Their duty to the settlement's wellbeing, their obligations to endow the Church, and the pressing need to save themselves from economic disaster, conjured up salvation on four hooves. Deliverance shone from the sheep's dull eye, and profit from its back as wool exports boomed.

By June 1853 Canterbury had 100 sheep runs over an area of a million acres. By the end of the following year all the plains and front slopes of the foothills were taken and, by 1856, most of the high country, merinos dribbling into the long, hard valleys of the Southern Alps. In 1851 there were just 15,000 sheep but a decade later Canterbury led the nation with a third of New Zealand's total flock of 2.7 million.

At about that time Samuel Butler, author of Erewhon, was exploring the alpine valleys, looking for new sheep country and in a tributary of the Rakaia River he gave the landscape typical pioneer treatment. He thought that the 'bush, though very beautiful to look at, is composed of nothing but the poorest black birch.' So he set it on fire '. . . and made a smoke which was noticed between fifty and sixty miles off. I have seen no grander sight than the fire upon a country which has never before been burnt . . . The sun loses all brightness, and looks as though seen through smoked glass'. Butler admitted, 'Our object was commercial not scientific; our motive was pounds, shillings and pence.'[2]

Steam locomotive at Lyttelton Tunnel, c. 1900.

G-1515-1/4, Alexander Turnbull Library, Wellington, New Zealand

Jack Suckling's Speedy Cycle Works,
Manchester Street, Christchurch. Jack
Suckling is standing in the centre of
the cyclists wearing a cap, watch and
chain, c. 1914.

G-24016-1/1, Alexander Turnbull Library, Wellington, New Zealand.

The fires of the sheepfarmers swept over the entire plains and foothills of the Southern Alps, incinerating most of the native plant cover, destroying entire bird species such as the native quail, completing the alteration of the vegetative cover begun by Maori centuries before. Sheep continued the change as they grazed over the landscape like maggots on a decaying carcase and exotic mammals such as rabbits were let loose to finish the job. Scores of un-named animal and plant species were lost and many others placed under threat. In concert with the burning of the runs, axe, saw and fire played like an apocalyptic trio as the forests of Banks Peninsula and North Canterbury were felled to build the growing city of Christchurch. In 1851, the Peninsula was two-thirds covered in bush; by 1900 hardly a native tree was to be found across the lowland reaches of the province.

Sheep and timber were not the only roads to a quick return. As goldfields and the Australian market grew, the plains became a vast field for bonanza wheat cropping. The land was broken by horse and plough until the hot nor'westers took the soil away in clouds of dust, sweeping out to sea. A century passed before the robber ethics of the colonial frontier gave way to a more sustainable farming economy. By then the province had become established as the agricultural and pastoral heartland of the country.

Christchurch grew steadily as the market, retail and industrial centre for the province, reflecting country wealth and pride. Timaru was its minor counterpart for the sub-province of South Canterbury. Farming prosperity saw the building of Christchurch Cathedral, begun in the 1870s and completed in 1904. Cathedral, museum, Christ's College, provincial government buildings and university arose in matching English Gothic and, outside the four avenues of the city proper, suburbs spread to accommodate an increasing population of clerks, shopkeepers and industrial workers. While Christchurch and Canterbury even today project echoes of the English class system, the city also has an enduring reputation for labour politics and unionism springing from the other side of the railway tracks in the industrial south of the city.

Rail, steam and agricultural mechanisation gave Christchurch companies an early reputation for engineering expertise. In 1861, only ten years after the founding of the colony, and when the combined population of city and its port was merely 5000, the first sod was turned for a great tunnel through the hill from Christchurch to its harbour, Lyttelton. Seven years later one of the longest railway tunnels

George Bernard Shaw (1856–1950) and
Joseph James Kinsey (1852–1936) at
'Warrimoo', the home of Sir Joseph,
Papanui Rd, Christchurch, 1934.

F-20830-1/2. Alexander Turnbull Library, Wellington, New Zealand.

in the world – at two and a half kilometres – was opened for traffic. A two-kilometre-long rail bridge across the Rakaia River was completed in 1873 as railways snaked out from Christchurch to bring people and produce from all corners of the province to market.

Through crop field and sheep paddock, through shelter belts of foreign pine, eucalypt and macrocarpa, long dusty rulers of roads also dissected the plains. In the late 1930s, Canterbury poet D'Arcy Cresswell wrote, 'The cars here travel very fast, in a great cloud of dust, and with no need of caution; which causes a constant rattle and uproar as the stones, being hurled in the air, strike on their windows and sides. With that travelling dust . . . and the heat and dryness in summer . . . the scene is Arabian almost . . . The plain has everywhere wonderful hues and a pallor and brightness of flame. The gum-trees . . . gleam and shine like the opal of many tints . . . As these disappear, then all at once the mountains are seen, near at hand.'[3]

Beyond the plains, the rough and dusty roads wind into the foothills and mountain uplands, a region that soon became known as the 'High Country', inhabited only by sheep-station owners, musterers with their amazing dogs and visited occasionally by mad mountaineers. Isolated in the grand and austere landscape beneath the craggy and icy alps, the runholders' lives and exploits became the stuff of pioneering legend. One of the most enduring New Zealand myths is of James Mackenzie and his dog who, in the 1850s, drove a mob of stolen sheep into the vast and secret basins of the lake country beneath Mount Cook. Mackenzie as hero symbolises the stoic pioneer man of the High Country but he also represents the colonial as rebel claiming his own piece of land. Mackenzie's collie bitch commands equal fame, representing all those wonderful sheep dogs that made open-range sheepfarming possible. The dog monument at Lake Tekapo in the Mackenzie Country attests to the enduring respect and gratitude of their owners.

There are three great roads into the High Country. The first and most spectacular was built to meet a gold rush when lucky strikes were made on the West Coast in 1864. A Maori pounamu trail from the Upper Waimakariri across the Main Divide was renamed Arthur's Pass, 900 metres in altitude, after its British rediscoverer. Within a year 1000 men with picks and shovels hacked more than 100 kilometres of coach road from the gorges and riverbeds. Prospectors from all over the world flooded over the pass, on foot or via a Cobb & Co. coach service started in 1866 that took thirty-six hours over a journey from Christchurch to Hokitika and

Double-decker tram in Cathedral Square,
Christchurch, c. 1900.

F-84695-1/2, Alexander Turnbull Library, Wellington, New Zealand.

included thirteen river crossings. Little gold was shipped back but Arthur's Pass provided the only transalpine road route for more than seventy years.

It became a train route also. The railway reached Springfield at the edge of the plains in 1880 and was worked through the Waimakariri gorge country to reach the site of the current Arthur's Pass village in 1914. By then, work had been in progress for six years on boring a tunnel under the Main Divide to Otira. A continuous rail route from Christchurch to Greymouth, Hokitika and Westport was finally completed in 1923.

The transalpine route via Arthur's Pass became important not only as a commercial connection but also as the road to mountain recreation and tourism. The tunnel workers' huts became the basis of an alpine village, winter day trips by train became popular, and the first skis were used on the slopes above Arthur's Pass in 1927. The region became the Mecca for young Canterbury mountaineers who tested their ice axes on Mount Rolleston before moving on to the big peaks further south. In 1929, Arthur's Pass National Park was established, the third in New Zealand.

My own first encounter with mountains, as a young man, was a vision of spring snow sparkling beneath a full moon on the peaks above the upper Waimakariri Valley. Bewitched and awed, I became a child of the mountains and nothing seemed more virtuous or valuable than to explore and understand the face of a high landscape. Among the Waimakariri's headwaters, I learned to ford its turbulent streams, to find a safe way over steep and shattered rock, to fashion a secure path through snow and ice with unfamiliar tools. The climbing rope brought friendship; bivouacs and huts the skills to live simply. The peaks brought the crystallisation of growing strength and confidence, the slow welding of a bond between myself and the mountains and a deepening understanding of both.

Those early journeys were full of trepidation when dangers loomed larger than they were. Exhaustion and despair always lay in wait and the toughening of nerve and muscle was never easy. I failed many times to reach summits, success often snatched away by wind and rain; but, in the end, rewards were sweeter for perseverance.

Children near the lighthouse in Lyttelton Harbour, 1882.

F-27866-1/2, Alexander Turnbull Library, Wellington, New Zealand.

After the Second World War, diesel railcars reduced the rail journey time from Christchurch to Arthur's Pass to less than three hours. The West Coast Highway was progressively sealed beyond Springfield after 1960 and re-engineered bridges and cuttings culminated in the 2000 opening of the splendid viaduct sweeping down the Otira Gorge. Improvement of the road brought much of the Canterbury High Country within a few hours' drive of Christchurch and stimulated the development of skifields such as Porter Heights and Craigieburn in adjacent sub-alpine basins. The Canterbury skiing industry began to boom in the 1960s following the development of the Mount Hutt basins above the Rakaia River, only an hour and a half's drive from the city.

Tourism and recreation also brought about the improvement of the second major highway through the High Country. The Lewis Pass route across the Southern Alps in North Canterbury was completed in 1937, providing an alternative way to Buller and Nelson. It winds through the most splendid beech forests in the South Island and gives access to the St James Walkway, opened in 1981, a memorable four-day tramp through sub-alpine forests and high-station country. The Lewis Pass highway also gives rapid access to the thermal district of Hanmer Springs. The first tourists to Hanmer bathed in pools surrounded by clumps of tussock and flax. Today it is a spa resort, with therapies to massage the mind and body and outdoor pursuits that range from pony rambling to mountain-bike hurtling. Along the way to Hanmer now you can try the Weka Pass vintage train ride after sampling the produce of the Waipara vineyards.

The third road to the High Country from the Canterbury Plains and downlands runs from its 'capital' – the country town of Fairlie – and over Burke's Pass, not to the West Coast but to the fabled Mackenzie Country and its icy lakes – Tekapo, Pukaki and Ohau. The Mackenzie basin never falls below 300 metres in altitude, stretches for 120 kilometres north to south, and cradles a host of snow-fed rivers that flow together as the great Waitaki ('Weeping Waters') on which the country's biggest earth dam and hydro-electric system are situated. Dams bar the rivers, new lakes have been formed, old lake levels raised to generate electricity for the power-hungry populations of the east coast and North Island. Pylons like skeletal giants stride over a landscape where aeons ago acres of ice carved away the land for the powdery blue lakes and swift grey rivers. The evidence of glacial grinding is still clear – chiselled mountainsides, terraces above the lakes and moraine hillocks beside concrete dams. Maori made

1489 - LIGHTHOUSE - LYTTLETON.

Ted and Grace Porter with their daughter Shirley and their son Robert on the Manuka Point Station, 1943.

C-8812-1/2, Alexander Turnbull Library, Wellington, New Zealand.

seasonal visits to the Mackenzie lakes to hunt waterfowl and other birds but the land had all been taken up for sheepfarming by the mid-1860s. By 1882, the Irish–Swiss team that made the first attempt on Mount Cook could take a train to Fairlie and a coach to Tekapo. But from there the journey was still by horse and waggon over the high downs to Mount Cook Station followed by a perilous crossing of the Tasman River which regularly consumed horses and drays. The team climbed within ten metres of the Himalayan-scale summit but patriots consider that the first real ascent of Mount Cook was made by home-grown Kiwis who spread a sugarbag on the top on Christmas Day 1894.

By that time they could stay (or work) at The Hermitage hotel and there was a rough shingle road from Tekapo to Pukaki ferry and then down the side of the lake to the foot of the great mountain. The Hermitage became the focus of New Zealand's high climbing and mountain tourist industry. All of New Zealand's outstanding guides and amateur climbers have made their reputations on the thirty 3000-metre peaks within what became known as Mount Cook National Park in 1953 – and celebrated their feats with a toast at The Hermitage bar. Sir Edmund Hillary made his first ascent of Mount Cook in 1947 with top guide Harry Ayres and went on to complete new climbs with Ayres before venturing to Everest. The scale of the park's glaciated high peaks made them an ideal training ground for the Himalaya, and New Zealand ice climbers were without peer in the mountains of Nepal and India during the 1950s and 1960s.

We stopped before the icy turret of the east Minaret. Sweat and snow cream had congealed over my nose, the goggles bit into my cheeks and my neck was smarting red from the ice-reflected sun. With a glance at the others, I stepped up and began chipping at the unblemished curve of dazzling snow that led to the summit. Higher, my head topped a ridge and my breath caught in my throat as I suddenly looked into an abyss of evil rock and swirling mist. If I should simply slip . . .

With extra care I began cutting steps up the narrow cone until, near the delicate wafer crest, I shaped a platform from which I could safeguard the others. As I pulled in the rope, they cramponned up carefully then paused beneath me on precarious holds. The wind was now stronger and our shouts of exultation were blown away.

A painting class from the School of Arts at the University of Canterbury, at the foot of the Cashmere Hills, near the Cracroft Bridge, Hoonhay, 1907.

G-5359-1/1, Alexander Turnbull Library, Wellington, New Zealand.

When I lifted my goggles, I looked out over a maze of blinding ice, wild jagged ridges and black chasms. To the west, the Tasman Sea was hidden by tumbling cloud; to the east Lake Pukaki and the Mackenzie Country seemed incongruously clear and calm and flat. To the south, Aoraki/Mount Cook bulked large but was the cornerpost of mountains far greater in the sum. I filled my lungs with the thin and icy alpine air. It was good to be alive, just to stand there for a moment on such a primeval stage, to feel the joy of having striven with body and mind through difficulties to reach such a simple but spectacular end.

Travel to the Hermitage moved from stage coach to open tourer car, to omnibus to plane and private car over roads that were eventually developed into the fastest highways in New Zealand. The challenges of this high mountain landscape also spurred the development of two machines that were to travel the world and reaffirm the skills of Canterbury engineers. On the rivers of Irishman Creek Station, Sir William Hamilton created the jetboat, capable of navigating the shallowest and most fast-running rivers, that went on to storm the Grand Canyon and the Ganges. And at Mount Cook, Sir Harry Wigley perfected a retractable ski-landing system for light planes, and mountain-flying techniques that enabled tourists, skiers and climbers to penetrate the most remote corners of the Alps.

Once upon a time the Mackenzie Country was synonymous with distance and silence but now there is no corner that is free for long from the sound of engines: of cars, trucks and tourist buses down the black-ribbon highways; of ski-plane, passenger plane and helicopter converging about the nexus of alpine valleys beneath Aoraki/Mount Cook; of jetboats on the lakes and rivers, four-wheel-drive vehicles on the riverbeds and farm tracks. The brown and treeless downs and basins have been transformed by plantation, irrigation and chemicals; the rabbit that once devastated this country has been fixed with a virus. Cattle have become more profitable than sheep, but the real wealth of the Mackenzie lies in tourism, whether sightseeing through a video camera or adventure tourism in a landscape that offers white and still water, ice, snow and vertiginous rock, fishing, hunting and some of the best gliding skies in the world.

Canterbury is now thoroughly settled and civilised and Christchurch, with a population of 330,000, has become the South Island's largest city, exceeded in size only by Auckland and greater Wellington. Its international airport is the base for the biggest Antarctic

Fair on Lyttelton wharf, c. 1914.

G-8563-1/1, Alexander Turnbull Library, Wellington, New Zealand.

supply operation in the world, the US military planes of 'Deep Freeze' linking with American and New Zealand bases on the ice throughout the southern summer.

With Christchurch and Canterbury, there is a merging of identity between town and country that makes the province a state within a state. Canterbury can be seen as the most complete expression of the colonising achievement in New Zealand: planned and orderly, a developed, democratic society that has found a balance between the urban and the rural, between agriculture and industry.

From a western slope of Banks Peninsula you may look out to city, plain, foothill and mountain, even to Aoraki/Mount Cook as it catches the sunrise; as an easterly shifts early fog, or the first warm stir of a nor'wester promises the march of a southerly front in its wake. Easterly, northerly, southerly, perhaps all in one day. Frost, thin rain, snow contracting or growing in the distance. Rivers thick with spring melt or narrowed by winter ice. The sea, the sky, the land – for more than 150 years, Canterbury.

---

1. Wall, Arnold, 'The Pioneers' from *The Pioneers and Other Poems*. A. H. & A. W. Reed, Wellington, 1948.
2. Butler, Samuel, *A First Year in Canterbury Settlement*. Rev. T. Butler, London, 1863.
3. Cresswell, D'Arcy, *Present Without Leave*. Cassell, London, 1939.

Farmland in the vicinity of Geraldine.

First light at Manuka Bay near Cheviot.

Wetlands in the Ahuriri Valley.

(Following pages) The fertile Canterbury
Plains were created by river systems carrying
huge amounts of silt and shingle down from
the Southern Alps. The Rakaia River is the
largest one.

Shunting of an historic steam locomotive at
Arthur's Pass station.

The small settlement of Arthur's Pass is largely made up of little cottages, where railway workers lived during construction of the Otira tunnel.

Morning frost covers Castle Hill Station.

Broken River cuts through layers of
limestone in Castle Hill basin. (Opposite)

The Castle Hill area was known as Kura Tawhiti and regarded as a place of spiritual significance.

Fishing hut at Lake Lyndon.

Bealey Bridge spans the Waimakariri River near Arthur's Pass.

(Following pages) The Torlesse Range separates Castle Hill basin from the Canterbury Plains to the east.

At Deans Bush, near the centre of
Christchurch, ancient Kahikatea trees
grow in a native bush setting.

The Port Hills above Christchurch, on the northern edge of Banks Peninsula, are widely used for recreation and accessible via the Summit Road.

Statue of John Robert Godley, the founder of
Canterbury.

Sculpture by Bing Dawe in the grounds of the
Arts Centre. (Opposite)

Punting on the Avon River past the Antigua
Boat Sheds, built in 1882.

New Regent Street was built in 1932, in Spanish Mission style.

Hedge sculpture at Mount Somers.

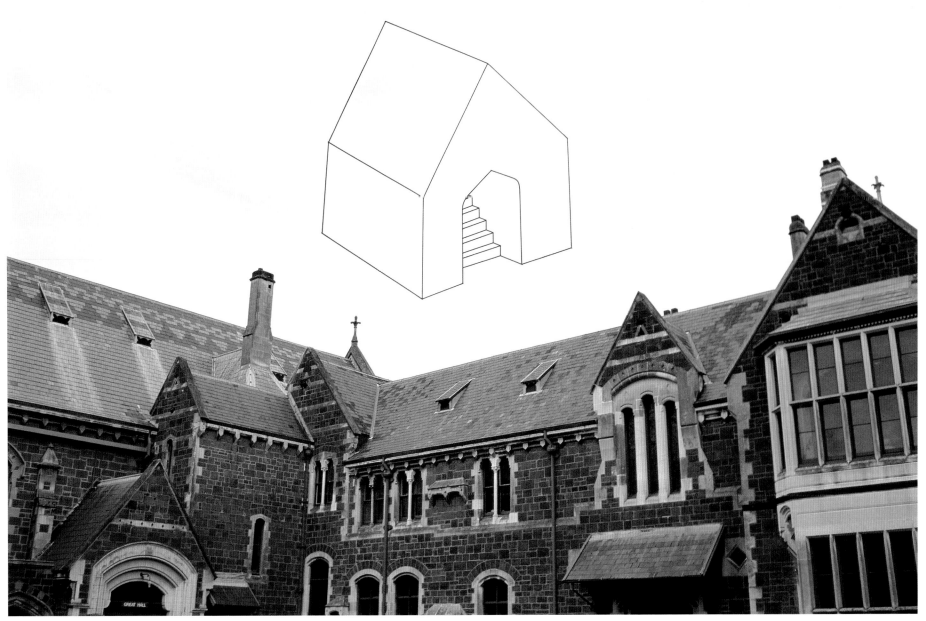

A modern sculptural echo, by Neil Dawson, of 19th century architecture at the Christchurch Arts Centre.

Cranmer Courts now houses apartments
behind the Gothic facades of Christchurch's
former Normal School.

View through the entrance of 'Sign of the Takahe'. Originally planned as a staging point along the Summit Road, the ornate building now houses a restaurant.

The Gothic stone buildings of the former University of Canterbury are now occupied by the Christchurch Arts Centre, a complex of shops, studios and galleries that also include the Court Theatre and Academy Cinema. (Opposite)

(Previous pages) 'Chalice' by sculptor Neil
Dawson in Cathedral Square, Christchurch.

The Provincial Council Chamber is New
Zealand's finest example of High Victorian
Gothic revival style.

Rugby training on a winter evening in
Hagley Park.

Red and black signify the spirit
of Canterbury rugby.

The recently built Christchurch Art Gallery
houses one of New Zealand's most important
public art collections.

The New Brighton Pier. The first pier on this
site was built in 1894.

View from Mountford Estate Wines over the
vineyards of North Canterbury's Waipara Valley.

Pegasus Bay Winery produces a wide variety of wines including Pinot Noir and Chardonnay.

Sunrise over a newly established vineyard in Waipara.

View over Kaikoura Peninsula towards South Bay.

The Seaward Kaikoura Range forms
an impressive backdrop to the wild
Kaikoura coast.

Whaling stopped in Kaikoura in the 1920s,
but whales are now the main attraction in
a thriving tourism industry.

Fyffe House at Avoca Point was part of the original whaling station. It has been preserved as the town's oldest dwelling.

Coastline at Hurunui River mouth.

Farmland around Cheviot.

A tree overlooking Manuka Bay adapted to
the prevailing south-west wind. (Opposite)

Cathedral Rocks above Gore Bay.

Okains Bay, Banks Peninsula:
Maori carving in the museum's
meeting house.

A waka tied up on the eve of Waitangi
Day celebrations. (Opposite)

The Summit Road winds along the crests of the two long-extinct volcanoes that form Banks Peninsula.

The small settlement of Okains Bay. (Opposite)

(Previous pages) Its many bays make Banks Peninsula a favourite recreation area for Christchurch residents.

Lyttelton Harbour.

A lavender farm on the outskirts of Akaroa contributes to its French charm.

Akaroa wharf. The atmosphere of the old
French colony lingers on.

Bull Kelp washed ashore on Kaitorete Spit.

The wild coast along Kaitorete Spit which separates Lake Ellesmere from the sea.

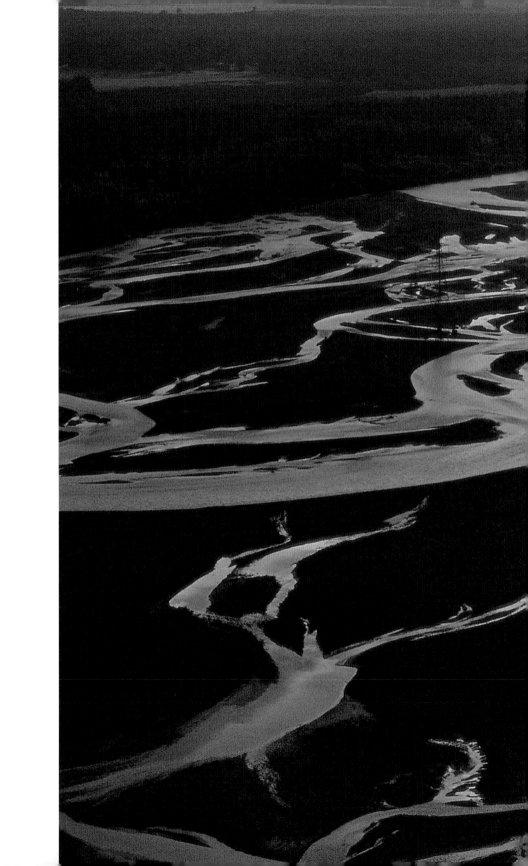

Rising in Arthur's Pass National Park,
the Waimakariri River crosses the
Canterbury Plains and meets the Pacific
north of Christchurch.

Macrocarpa hedges protect Canterbury Plains farmlands from the region's strong winds. (Opposite)

Crop farmers prepare the fertile soil for the next growing cycle.

(Following page) Autumn sunrise over farmland around Barrhill.

Longbeach, near the Ashburton River, was once described as the world's best farm. Many buildings of the self-contained village are still in use.

The Canterbury Plains form the largest
lowland area in New Zealand.

Stony Plains soils do not deter farmers
from creating fine gardens. Garden inspired
by Monet at Stonehaven farm near Mayfield.
(Opposite)

War memorial in Timaru. (Opposite)

The homestead on Northdown Farm near Timaru is made of rammed earth and dates back to 1868.

Historic buildings in Waimate tell stories of a rich past.

View over the foothills of Inverary Station
towards the Mount Somers range.

From the Southern Alps the snow-fed
Rakaia River flows from it's gorge and
across the plains.

A flock of geese change feeding grounds after
the sun has set.

The Rangitata River mouth is famous for its salmon fishery and for sea-run brown trout.

Houses of a small fishing village at
Lake Clearwater.

Potts River, a tributary to the
Rangitata River.

(Following pages) Lake Stream joins the
Rakaia River on its 145-kilometre journey to
the Pacific.

Autumn muster at Lake Heron Station.

Willows at the outlet of Lake McGregor
near Tekapo.

Cattle adapt well to the harsh conditions of
High Country weather and have replaced
traditional flocks of sheep on some stations.

Homestead at Drycreek Station near Fairlie.

Autumn muster of Merino sheep in the Lake Waitaki area.

View from Mount Sunday towards the
Potts Range and one of the highest
commercial skifields in Canterbury.

Stormy weather on Highway 8 near Fairlie signals the onset of winter. (Opposite)

Bathers enjoy a crisp winter morning at Hanmer Springs Thermal Resort.

Hanmer Plain after a fresh snowfall.

Hoar frost coats autumn grass.

Sheep feeding out on snow-covered hills
above Fairlie.

Moa statues built by the Alford Forest community under the direction of sculptor Clive Seddon.

Lake Tekapo in the Mackenzie Basin.

Showers over the Benmore Range near
Twizel. (Opposite)

View from Mount John over Lake Tekapo
towards the Two Thumb and Sibbald ranges.

View across Lake Pukaki towards
Aoraki/Mount Cook.

The Church of the Good Shepherd was built in 1935 to commemorate pioneering Mackenzie Country families.

Many glacier-fed streams in the Hooker
Valley provide good growing conditions for
the Mount Cook Lily, the largest buttercup
in the world.

Mueller Glacier Lake above Mount Cook Village.

High winds blow snow over the Main Divide
between Mount Brunner and Mount Sefton.

Aoraki/Mount Cook (3754 metres), New
Zealand's highest peak, seen from the
shores of Lake Pukaki.

The big lakes of the Mackenzie Country feed
the Upper Waitaki hydro-electric power scheme.

Hydro channels are sought-after
fishing spots.

(Following page) Autumn mist on Lake Tekapo.

View over Lake Alexandrina towards the Hall and Gammack ranges. (Opposite)

Holiday home on the lake shore.

Lake Alexandrina is known for its great trout fishing.

(Previous page) Limestone formations at Castle Hill.

Last light near Irishman Creek Station in the Mackenzie Country.

TECHNICAL NOTES   The film of my choice for this book was Fuji Velvia RVP, which I rated at 80 ASA and push-processed by one f-stop. For some images I used Fuji Provia 100F to obtain less-saturated colours.

All my films were developed by Labtec Photographic Processing Limited.

I worked with two camera formats; Nikon cameras and lenses for 35 mm film and a Mamiya 7 rangefinder camera for 120 format. Wide-angle lenses are my work-horses, the Nikon 24 mm and the Mamiya 43 mm rate among my favourite ones.

VIKING An imprint of Penguin Books
Penguin Books (NZ) Ltd,
cnr Rosedale and Airborne Roads, Albany,
Auckland 1310, New Zealand
Penguin Books Ltd,
80 Strand, London, WC2R 0RL, England
Penguin Group (USA) Inc.,
375 Hudson Street, New York, NY 10014, United States
Penguin Books Australia Ltd, 250 Camberwell Road,
Camberwell, Victoria 3124, Australia
Penguin Books Canada Ltd,
10 Alcorn Avenue, Toronto, Ontario, Canada M4V 3B2
Penguin Books (South Africa) (Pty) Ltd,
24 Sturdee Avenue, Rosebank, Johannesburg 2196, South
Africa
Penguin Books India (P) Ltd,
11, Community Centre, Panchsheel Park,
New Delhi 110 017, India

Penguin Books Ltd, Registered Offices: 80 Strand, London,
WC2R 0RL, England

First published in 2005

1 3 5 7 9 10 8 6 4 2

Copyright © text, Philip Temple, 2005
Copyright © illustrations, Arno Gasteiger, 2005
Thanks to Reed Publishing (NZ) Ltd for permission to
publish from Arnold Wall's 'The Pioneers of Canterbury'.

The rights of Philip Temple and Arno Gasteiger
to be identified as the authors of this work in
terms of section 96 of the Copyright Act 1994 is
hereby asserted.

All rights reserved. Without limiting the rights under
copyright reserved above, no part of this publication may
be reproduced, stored in or introduced into a retrieval
system, or transmitted, in any form or by any means
(electronic, mechanical, photocopying, recording or
otherwise), without the prior written permission of both
the copyright owner and the above publisher of this book.

Designed by Athena Sommerfeld
Prepress by microdot
Printed in China through Bookbuilders, Hong Kong

ISBN 0 67 004555 1
A catalogue record for this book is available
from the National Library of New Zealand.

www.penguin.co.nz